Viking Product Launching Page

Chapter 1:

Introduction to Product Launching

So, what does every guru online tell you to do if you want to grow your internet marketing business? Give away lead magnets to freebie-seekers. Build your list. Market affiliate products to them. Make commissions. We've all heard it, right? And you know what? That strategy worked. Back in 2012...

Problem is, it doesn't work anymore. Nowadays, freebie-seekers have secondary "junk" email accounts that they reserve for collecting lead magnets but otherwise they never log in to them. Your emails are going to inboxes where they are left untouched, floating in a sea of thousands of other marketing emails. This, combined with the fact that many people even use fake email addresses, is what has led to such severely low email open rates throughout the industry. And not only does a list of freebie-seekers almost never open your emails, but the few of them that do will almost never buy anything. Why? Because they're freebie-seekers!

So, what is it that successful internet marketers are doing differently? They're each building a "super list". A super list (phrase coined by the great Alex Jeffreys), is a list of real people, with real email addresses that they actually check, who actually habitually take out their credit cards and buy things online. In other words, it's a buyers list. The difference between a buyers list and a freebie-seeker list is night and day. One makes you money and the other makes you angry.

So how do you get a buyers list? Easy. You launch a product and you get affiliates to send traffic to it. Then you simply integrate your payment platform with your autoresponder service so that buyers get added as subscribers automatically. Don't worry. It's not as crazy as it sounds and, more importantly, it's the only way you'll move forward in internet marketing.

Now we should note that this guide assumes you've already got a core product created. It's okay if you don't have a sales structure set up yet, such as sales pages, a funnel, or a member's area, because we'll cover all that next. But at a minimum we're assuming you've already got a product created, whether it be an eBook, a video course, or a software tool. If you haven't created a product yet, just grab our Product Creation guide which will have you cranking out digital products in no time.

How Do You Launch a Product?

There are a few ways to launch a digital product. One way is to do a "soft launch". A soft launch is a low-key opening of the doors, so to speak. You set up a product, have it ready to accept sales, and instead of having a major announced launch period with special promotions, you simply start sending traffic to it.

On the other hand, there's a "hard launch". A hard launch is a publicized launch period with a specific beginning and end date. The idea here is to drive large amounts of traffic to your new product in a short period of time. In most cases, there's a special discount during this short period which encourages people to adopt the product early. Ultimately, the goal of a hard launch is to bring in a large number of new customers (and revenue) and to make a very visible splash in the marketplace.

Since the goal of this guide is to get you a buyers list as quickly as possible, we'll be focusing on how to accomplish a hard launch.

The most important "how" of your product, however, is traffic. Where will you get it? You certainly COULD drive your own traffic with paid ads and hope that you make a profit, but the most popular approach is to recruit affiliates (also called

"JVs"). If you can convince and incentivize several affiliate marketers who already have their own audiences and email lists to promote your product, you're basically handing off the problem of traffic generation to someone else. It's also great because you don't have to worry about spending your own money in advance. You're simply paying commissions using money from sales that were already made by the affiliates. You also have the benefit of not having to worry about targeting and tweaking and other stuff you have to mess with when you pay for your own traffic. All the people on these affiliate marketers' lists are already interested in your niche and are likely already habitual buyers of products like yours. So, for the purposes of this guide, we'll be focusing on getting a bunch of JVs/affiliates to promote a hard launch. But before we start recruiting JVs and sending traffic, you'll need to set up your launch structure and that's what we'll be covering next.

Chapter 2:

Building Your Launch Structure

Before you start recruiting JVs and sending traffic to a hard launch, you'll need your actual launch structure in place. Your launch structure includes your sales pages, your sales funnel, your pricing model, as well as the marketplace or payment platform you'll use.

Your launch structure also includes the backend infrastructure you'll need for delivering your products to buyers and your initial interactions with them after they purchase. This includes setting up a support desk, a member's area (or product delivery apparatus), and an autoresponder welcome sequence. (Note: many would argue that these last three items are better categorized as CRM rather than part of your launch structure, and that's a valid point, but we're dealing specifically with the immediate post-purchase interactions that often make the difference between happy customers and angry refunders, so we've included them as part of your launch structure). Let's take a closer look at each of these.

Sales Funnel

Before you start building the pages, you'll need to establish your funnel flow. Hopefully you've done a good job of splintering your product into multiple stand-alone components or combining your product with other relevant products. The reason you need to do this is so that you'll have multiple products to upsell and downsell through a funnel in order to maximize your revenue. If you haven't done this yet or aren't sure how, see our guide on Product Creation.

The flow of your sales funnel basically handles what happens after a person buys your front-end product. Ordinarily, they'll be offered a relevant, higher-priced product as an upsell. This product should ideally augment or reinforce what the front-end product does. You'll then need to plan for a "yes or no" scenario. You'll (probably) want a second upsell in case the buyer purchases the first upsell, and you'll need a downsell if they decline it. This can theoretically go on as long as you want, but generally you'll annoy people if your sales funnel is more than 4, maybe 5 products deep. Depending on what marketplace you'll be using (discussed later), you'll be able to create product listings and set up your sales funnel before designing your actual sales pages.

Pricing

Finding the perfect pricing strategy for the products in your funnel can make a world of difference. First, you'll want to establish what your "normal" price will be after your launch period. In most cases, this will already be lower than your product's actual assessed value. But then, for your special launch period, you'll typically want to offer an even lower price to encourage early adopters. But be careful. This isn't a race to the bottom. Often times, a price that is too low will kill the perceived value of your product and can actually drive prospects away. You'll want to think long and hard about how to find the perfect "sweet spot" that maintains the perceived value of your product while also making it a no-brainer to snatch it up before the launch ends. Plan on a few different pricing ideas and combinations throughout your funnel so that, if you feel the offer isn't performing well, you can change it up. Be sure to be taking notes if/when you make changes so you can compare performance at various price points.

Marketplaces

The last component of your structure that needs to be established before moving on to the sales pages themselves is which marketplace or payment platform you'll be using. If you're relatively new to product launching and you're relying heavily on JVs, you'll want to stick with one of the big affiliate marketplaces rather than your own payment platform. This is because you'll have a greater chance of attracting affiliates and many of these marketers are only comfortable with these marketplaces anyway. The reason this decision should come before your actual pages is that some of these marketplaces have specific guidelines and requirements for vendors and their pages. For a long time, ClickBank was the preeminent, go-to affiliate marketplace for digital goods. In recent years, however, JVZoo has emerged as an even more popular marketplace for hard launches. ClickBank has the benefit of being a little easier to use from an affiliate point of view because most products don't require you to wait for the vendor to manually approve you as an affiliate. However, ClickBank is also much stricter in its guidelines for vendors and their pages and they also seem to be more evergreen oriented than launch oriented. JVZoo, on the other hand, is much more launch oriented and seems to be the preferred affiliate marketplace for both vendors and affiliates when it comes to launching new products. Another marketplace worth mentioning is WarriorPlus. This one is not necessarily "new" but it's been recently updated and expanded and is making a big comeback. It seems to have more in common with JVZoo than ClickBank and is very much associated with the Warrior Forum community (although the two are not officially or legally the same). Whichever marketplace you choose, be sure to carefully review their vendor guidelines and familiarize yourself with their policies.

Sales Pages

It doesn't matter if you know you have the most amazing, valuable, life-changing product in the world. If your sales page isn't converting, you won't succeed. Your sales pages act as a sort of bottleneck of your product's success. There are a lot of different approaches to sales pages and copy. Short-form, long-form, text-only, video-only, and so on. The most common one's you'll see today are hybrid mid- to long-form video sales letters. This means a sales page in which the center of attention is a sales video at the top, under a headline, and then a long or medium length sales letter below it that basically repeats the message of the video. This type of page has the advantage of appealing to people who people who like to learn via video, people who like to learn by reading thoroughly, and people who like to just skim down the page and collect the main ideas. Whatever style you choose, make sure you keep it clean looking, attractive, and have every element and aspect of it point towards your main goal: the buy button. Buy buttons, headlines, and CTAs should be clear and pop-out easily from the background (so ensure you use contrasting colors). The overall look and feel of your sales page should ideally match the theme and colors of your brand image. Ideally, a page like this will have lots of images and sub-headlines to break up the text. Because a sales page is such a vital part of your success, it's something you should really consider outsourcing if you aren't already good at it.

Product Delivery and Membership

So, once you've collected a payment, you'll need an automated method to deliver the product to your buyer. Some marketplaces provide product download or delivery within their platform. Alternatively, you can just forward buyers to your own delivery page with download links or the video lessons and so on. But it's best, these days, to take an extra step towards protecting your content and to lock it behind a members' area. There are several options for this. First, there are the more common WordPress-based options like WishlistMember, MemberMouse, and Digital Access Pass. Then, there are non-WordPress solutions like Kajabi or FreshMember. Whichever you choose, you'll need to go through a few steps to integrate it with your payment platform or marketplace so that people can automatically access their purchases after buying. Also, pay close attention to how you're setting up your membership script and ensure that it's protecting all the correct pages for all the correct products. Also, test to make sure login details are automatically being sent at the moment of purchase. Another important benefit to membership-based delivery is that it can decrease refund rates. If unscrupulous customers have to login to access materials, they're less likely to request their money back than if they can simply download files to their computer right away.

Customer Support

Customer support will be a permanent part of your relationship with each of your customers. However, for this guide, we're specifically focused on the very first interaction you'll be having with each customer. Namely, login headaches and refunds. Prior to your launch, ensure you've picked out and tested a solid support desk software. There are many out there to choose from. The two most popular ones are arguably ZenDesk and FreshDesk. Try a couple out and see which ones work best for you or your agents if you employ support staff. Once you've got your helpdesk setup, you'll want to establish streamlined workflows and canned statements specifically for dealing with things like refunds and login problems. You can guarantee you'll have a lot of both of these. Your canned response for refunds can either be to oblige immediately or to offer a "bribe" of some sort first to keep the refund-requester on-board. For login issues, you'll want a step-by-step process of immediately looking up a person's transaction to verify what they bought, then looking up their account information in your membership platform and either resending credentials or creating new ones. Also consider putting important info into your helpdesk's autoresponse. Rather than "we've received your ticket and will review it shortly" consider adding a few things like "if you haven't received login details, please check your spam folder" and "due to our current product launch, support tickets may take a full 48 hours".

Welcome Sequence

A full post-launch email autoresponder sequence will be covered later on. Right now we want to focus on the welcome sequence. Also called an indoctrination sequence, what you want to do is immediately greet and welcome the new customer with an email message. In this message you'll want to footstomp a few things such as asking them to whitelist your email address (include a link to a whitelisting tutorial), reminding them to check their spam for important product access information, a little introduction about your business and what they can expect to hear from you in the future, and finally, a cliff-hanger. The cliffhanger is a promise of something, relevant to what they just bought, that will be sent to them the following day. The next day you can send out a relevant email with info about how to use their product or tips and tricks, and so on. The day after that, you can introduce them to your most popular blog content or something. It doesn't really matter what you cover in these first few emails, as long as you're providing value and establishing a relationship. But there is one specific thing you'll want to consider doing for each of these welcome sequence emails. You'll want to include an invitation to purchase other products in the funnel, on the off chance the buyer declined your upsells. This can be a main point, emphasizing that the special launch price will soon expire, or it can be more subtle and simply added in the P.S. area.

Now that your sales structure itself is up and running, it's time to go get some affiliates and convince them to send their traffic to your offer.

Chapter 3:

Affiliate Recruitment

Why Recruit JVs/Affiliates?

There are plenty of ways to drive traffic today. But generally, when you need to drive large amounts of it for a product launch, you'll be using paid methods. In many industries, the standard is, of course, paid advertising - usually pay-per-click or PPC. This is risky because you are paying out money for traffic without a guarantee that those clicks you paid for will convert to sales. So you're risking loss and you have little or no control of what your ROI will be.

For example, you might pay $200 for 200 clicks and only make $210 from the handful of sales you made. It's great that you at least broke even, but you had no control over that outcome and in the next campaign you might make back less than you spent. You can still make this model work, obviously, but it requires a lot of testing, tweaking, adjusting, and a ton of "ad spend" just to get to the point where you've optimized and gained better control over your expected ROI.

Compare that to the JV/affiliate model. When you do a JV-driven product launch, you don't have to worry about ad spend. You're only paying for successful sales after they happen and you know in advance what amount you're paying per sale. You also don't have to spend any time or money testing and tweaking and targeting. You're handing all that hard work over to JVs with their own lists and audiences that they already know well and know how to pitch and market to.

When you compare the two, clearly the JV/affiliate model holds an advantage, especially if you're an independent entrepreneur and not a business with a huge advertising budget. Bottom line: if you want to launch a digital product, you need JVs sending traffic to your offer or you can kiss your dreams of having a big buyers list goodbye.

What to Pay Them

If a buyers list is your priority, rather than profit – and it should be – then the indisputable best commission rate is 100%. 100% commission launches automatically pop out and appear more attractive when JVs are looking at upcoming launches. Remember, your launch is not the only one out there, vying for affiliates. If an affiliate can make more money with other launches, he or she will ignore yours. So, if your front-end product is less than $20, you should seriously consider 100% commissions (you can always drop it to 50% after the launch). If your front-end product is higher than $20, then it is acceptable to offer something like 50% or 75%. The most common commission rate for the rest of a funnel is 50%.

Where to Recruit

Launch announcement sites are an excellent place to let JVs know about your upcoming launch. The two most popular ones are Muncheye and JV Notify. Both of these have a free level where you can list your upcoming launch. However, to get an extra edge, you might opt to pay for added exposure on these sites. Both of them have paid options that will cause your JV recruiting ads to be more prominent and get more views.

Another good place to advertise your launch is on the affiliate marketplaces themselves. JVZoo, ClickBank, and WarriorPlus all have paid advertising options that will allow you to get your launch in front of potential JVs. The success rate and ROI of these advertisements will vary quite a bit.

You can also announce your launch in one of the many Facebook JV/launch announcement groups. These groups tend to be private, so you'll have to request to join each of them. There are literally a ton of these groups on Facebook. Many of these groups are like notice boards where everyone posts their launch but very few people read about launches, while others are much more interactive and fruitful. Since it only takes a moment to post in each of these, you might as well post even in the lower quality ones, but just be aware that results will vary.

A Note on Coaches as JVs

Arguably, the quickest and easiest way to get a high-level JV on your team is to join their coaching program. Many IM coaches offer to promote your product as part of their coaching package. However, you should typically do this well in advance of your launch or even in advance of your product creation. This is because these coaches desire to work with active students and do not want their coaching programs to become "affiliate for hire" programs. Coaching programs tend to be very expensive, but they are often, ironically, less expensive and more effective than the above-mentioned paid ads that people often spend a lot of money on.

A JV signup page is vital to getting affiliates on board and there are a ton of important elements that you should include, starting with a JV invite video. Your JV invite video is most effective if it features you in "talking head" format. You should describe your product thoroughly as well as all the details of your launch. This means you should mention your funnel and commission model, your contest and prizes, and so on. Ultimately your video should end by thanking JVs for considering your launch and repeating your invitation.

Your sales funnel diagram would typically be the same place you lay out your commission model. Ideally, you should have a graphical representation of each step in your funnel indicating all of the upsells and downsells along with the commission percentage for each of those steps and the price of each of those products. Include any different pricing options you have for each of those products. You may specify what each step or product is on this diagram or it is also acceptable to simply label them as OTO 1, 2, etc., but expect some JVs to contact you and ask what those OTOs are.

Usually your contest and leaderboard will be together in the same section. You'll want to show images of your contest prizes if they are physical items as well as other details (i.e. if you're offering cash alternatives for people who don't want the physical prizes). If you have minimum sales requirements for each prize, list those clearly. But be warned, a lot of JVs don't like minimum requirements.

As for the leaderboard, you'll want that posted above or below the contest info. You can manually update the leaderboard yourself periodically or you can use an embedding tool that automatically updates it based on the data from JVZoo, W+, etc. It is not necessary to show the number of sales the contestants are making on the leaderboard and most marketers keep this private.

You'll be wanting to update your JVs every day on how the launch is going and to encourage them to keep promoting. To do this, you'll need their email address. You should have an easily visible opt-in form for JVs to sign up. An added benefit of this is that on later launches you'll have a list of JVs that you can email and notify about your launches.

In order to make life easier on your JVs, encourage them to promote, and help them get higher conversions, you should provide done-for-you bonuses. These can simply be repurposed PLR/MRR content (check the licenses and make sure you can use them as bonuses) that you place into a zip file and provide a download link on the JV page. For a course on how to make these bonuses look gorgeous and appealing, see our Bonus Creation course.

Once you've got your bonuses, you'll want to go the extra mile and create a bonus template. This simply means creating an html or WP page with those bonuses on them, maybe some images and a few headlines about your product with a CTA stating "grab these bonuses when you buy [your product] through our link". You then place this into a zip file and your JVs can simply upload it to their website and drive traffic to that bonus page. You can either hire someone on Fiverr to create a basic page like this or use an easy web builder like OptimizePress 2.0 to build it yourself and export the page as an OP2 template (but keep in mind not all your JVs have OP2).

Just like you need to provide DFY bonuses and bonus pages to them, you also need to provide pre-written emails for them to use. You may find this hard to believe, but if you look closely at the promotional emails in your inbox and then look at the JV pages for those products, you'll notice that even famous, high-level marketers often use pre-written swipes from JV pages. Why? Because it takes time to write a good sales email and even more to fill your email marketing schedule with a whole series of them. Providing JVs with email swipes allows them to copy and paste promotional emails and simply tweak them a bit to make them more unique. I'm not saying ALL JVs care about email swipes, but for many of them, this definitely makes your launch more attractive. At a minimum, you should have one email for each day of your launch, but 2 per day is better and having 4 or 5 scarcity-based ones for the last 48 hours of launch is even better.

In this same section, you can also add an assortment of graphics and banners for people to use in their blogs, sites, and even paid ad campaigns. These are probably used less often, but it's still worth having them. If you aren't sure what sizes or dimensions to provide, you can simply go to Google's AdWords advertising site and look at their guidelines for banner ad sizes. This isn't because you're making these for google, but simply because they cover a broad range of shapes and sizes that can be useful anywhere.

To give your affiliates an idea of how attractive your offer will be to their audience, you'll want to add a preview of your sales page. This also allows them to read up on the basics of your product so they can understand it better and write more detailed and accurate promotional content about it.

Arguably the most important part, make sure you have a big, bright, prominent button on your page inviting affiliates to request an affiliate link for your product. This should link to your affiliate registration/details page on whichever affiliate platform or marketplace you're using. So now that you've got a launch date set and affiliates recruited, it's time to get ready for your first digital product launch.

Chapter 4:
The Launch

So, you've got a product, your date is set, your sales funnel is ready, and your army of affiliates is standing by. It's time to launch your product (but first, a quick note on pre-launches).

Pre-launch

One thing you might want to do in the days prior to launch is a pre-launch. Pre-launches are a little less common today than they used to be, but they can be super useful. Generally, a pre-launch just consists of a landing page where people can sign up to be notified of your launch and, ideally, you'll incentivize them with a special low price or early access or both. The idea here is that if you can get a significant amount of people interested in advance, get them committed, and get their email addresses, you'll be able to mail them and start your launch off with a boom. You'll want to ensure you've got your pre-launch landing page designated with your affiliate platform in a way that gives affiliates credit for anyone they send to the pre-launch page prior to launch.

Launch week

This is it. This is the moment you've been working towards all along. It's launch week. Hopefully you did a good job of communicating to your affiliates what time you want them to start mailing and hopefully you didn't make a rookie mistake like forgetting to set your product listing to "allow sales" or something. Now there are several things to keep in mind for launch week.

Firstly, make sure you make a good impression on your customers by keeping an eye on your help desk and answering tickets and fixing issues ASAP. Secondly, keep your affiliates up-to-date and motivated with regular updates about the JV leaderboard and the funnel's performance. Do this via email, social media, your blog, and so on. Third, it's tempting to stay up all day and all night watching the sales roll in or worrying about customer support issues (especially if there's something problematic happening with your membership or software) and yes, you'll likely not get as much sleep during a launch, but don't wear yourself out too much. Whether things are going really badly or really well, remember that life goes on. Make some time to hang out with your loved ones and be sure to get some good rest whenever able.

Post-launch

If you've had a particularly taxing launch, it's tempting to want to put your feet up and disappear for a few days afterwards. Not so fast... You've got important post-launch work to do. Firstly, you need to ensure you send out a big thank you message/post/video to all your affiliates. It's important to make them feel appreciated since you'll likely be relying on them again on the next launch. Then, ensure you pay out or ship off whatever prizes were won by the JVs on your leaderboard. Also make sure you go in and make any manual commission payments you still owe (e.g. with JVZoo your

Stripe transactions don't automatically "split" so you have to manually pay affiliates for those sales). Definitely don't forget to increase your product price. False scarcity makes people angry and causes a loss of credibility for you and your affiliates. If you said the launch price was going to end at midnight, you need to increase it after that. Finally, ensure you've got a robust autoresponder sequence scheduled to kick in for each buyer right after they finish your welcome/indoctrination series. Keep in mind, your buyers have a hundred other marketers bombarding their inboxes all day long, if you don't start your email marketing immediately after their purchase, they'll forget about you and will wonder who you are and how you got their email.

Evergreen

Just because your launch period has ended doesn't mean the doors are closed. On the contrary, you want to bring is as much consistent evergreen traffic as possible. Make a note on your JV page that you are now evergreen and encourage existing affiliates and future ones who may happen upon your page to plug your offer into their autoresponders as an evergreen product. Also, consider reaching out to affiliates for private promotion opportunities where you can put a message like "special offer for followers of so and so" at the top of the page and let their audience get the offer at the original launch price.

Everything you've learned here has the potential to get your business off the ground and your buyers list built in no time. But it'll have been completely useless if you don't start taking action right away. Put this guide to work by implementing the following battle plan today.

Battle Plan

Step 1: Determine which affiliate marketplace you'll be launching in and schedule your launch date.

Step 2: Draft up your funnel and pricing structure (splinter products, if necessary).

Step 3: Design or outsource your sales pages.

Step 4: Choose your help desk and product delivery method.

Step 5: Write out and schedule your welcome/indoctrination sequence in your autoresponder.

Step 6: Develop an affiliate signup page and start recruiting affiliates.

Step 7: Get ready for your first launch!